THE MAMMOTH BOOK OF
Native Americans

THE MAMMOTH BOOK OF
Native Americans

JON E. LEWIS

ROBINSON
London

Constable & Robinson Ltd
3 The Lanchesters
162 Fulham Palace Road
London W6 9ER
www.constablerobinson.com

First published in the UK by Robinson,
an imprint of Constable & Robinson Ltd 2004

A copy of the British Library Cataloguing in
Publication Data is available from the British Library

ISBN 978-1-84119-593-3

Printed and bound in the EU

6 7 8 9 10

For Freda, Tristram and Penny

Contents

Chronology

c. 30,000BC
First humans enter North America, via Bering land bridge

c. 8000BC
Ice Age ends; mastodon, giant horse, sabre-toothed tiger, miniature horse and other fauna become extinct

5000BC
Eskimo-Aleut and Na-Dene people migrate to North America from Asia

1500BC
Indians of the north-eastern woodlands adopt practice of burying their dead

1000BC
Maize becomes food staple of Mexican Indians; agriculture established in Mogollon highlands of American Southwest; the beginning of Adena culture

200–500AD
Hopewell civilization flourishes in Midwest and East

750AD
Mississippian Culture in ascendancy

850–1150
Zenith of City of Cahokia, on site of present day St Louis

800–1100
Maize becomes major crop in Eastern woodlands

900
Rise of Anasazi civilization in Southwest

c. 1000
Pueblo communities of Acoma and Hopi established

1075
Anasazi road-building begins at Chaco Canyon

c.1130
Anasazi evacuate Chaco Canyon

c.1450
Confederacy of the Iroquois born

1492
Columbus lands in Bahamas; population of North America as high as 18 million

1500
Algonquian-speaking nations push sedentary Iroquian people from the north-east

1513
Ponce de Leon lands in Florida

1521
Second Ponce de Leon expedition forced to evacuate Florida by Calusa tribes

1528
Panfilo de Narvaez lands at Tampa Bay, Florida, but retreats after Indian attacks

1539–43

Hernado de Soto lands in Florida and rampages westwards through the Timucua, Creek, Mobile, Apalachee and other nations; de Soto buried next to the Mississippi in 1542

1540–42

Francisco Vasquez de Coronado leads Spanish expedition from Mexico, penetrating as far north as Kansas.

1598

Juan de Onate founds Spanish settlements in northern New Mexico

1599

Vincente Zaldivar attacks Acoma ('Sky City') pueblo, killing 800

1600s

Navajo adopt sheep farming and the reintroduced horse (c.1659)

1607

English colonists establish permanent settlement at Jamestown, Virginia

1609–13

War between Powhatan and Jamestown settlers; peace sealed by marriage of Princess Pocahontas to John Rolfe

1609

Samuel de Champlain kills three Iroquois chiefs with a single bullet on shore of Lake Champlain

1612

Jesuits begin arriving in New France (Canada)

1617

Pocahontas dies on trip to England

1620
English Pilgrims land at Plymouth

1622
Opechancanough of the Powhatan attacks Virginian settlements (until 1632)

1637
Pequot War against English to maintain hunting grounds, Connecticut

1644
Second Opechancanough War sees demise of the Powhatan Confederacy

1650–1777
Iroquois Confederacy at height of influence

1663
Bible translated into Massachusetts ('Mamusse Wunneetupanatamwe Up-Biblum God Naneeswe Nukkone Testament Kah Wonk Wusku Testament') by John Eliot

1675–6
King Philip's War; after early successes, Wampanoags and Narragansetts slaughtered and enslaved

1680
Revolt of the Pueblos

c.1700
Comanche established on Southern Plains and horsed

1712
Tuscarora War in North Carolina

1731
French capture Great Sun of the Natchez and sell him into slavery

1737
'The Walking Purchase' defrauds the Delaware of twelve hundred square miles of land.

1738
Smallpox strikes the Missouri region causing 90 per cent mortality amongst the Arikara

1742
Joseph Brant (Thayendanegea) of the Mohawk born

1750
Plains Cree horsed

1754-63
French and Indian War ends in victory for Britain

1763
Pontiac's Rebellion, Great Lakes

1769
Spanish establish missions in California; over the next 60 years Native population of California between Dan Diego and San Francisco declines from seventy-two thousand to eighteen thousand through disease and forced labour

1770
Cheyenne horsed on Northern Plains

1775
Revolution begins

1777

Shawnee raids against white settlements in 'Kentucke' reach peak

1779

Retaliatory campaign by Generals Clinton and Sullivan raze 40 pro-British Iroquois towns in Mohawk Valley

1783

America granted independence from Britain

1786

Tlingit on NW coast first encounter whites

1791

Miami Chief Little Turtle inflicts 900 casualties on US force led by General St Clair; worst US defeat in any war against the Indians

1794

Ohio-region Indians lose Battle of Fallen Timbers

1795

Under terms of the Treaty of Greenville Indians forfeit slice of southern Indiana and most of Ohio

1799

Handsome Lake of the Seneca receives vision in which Jesus tells him 'Now tell your people that they will become lost when they follow the ways of the White man'

1800

Indian population estimated at 600,000 by Bureau of Indian Affairs

1803

Louisiana Purchase from France places 828,000 square miles of the trans-Mississippi and its tribes under US dominion

1804–6

'Voyage of Discovery' by Lewis and Clark to Pacific Ocean

1809–11

Tecumseh of the Shawnee campaigns for Native American unity; his brother and ally Tenkswatawa defeated at Tippecanoe, Indiana, by Governor Harrison

1812–15

War of 1812 between Britain and USA

1813

Tecumseh killed in battle of the Thames fighting alongside British

1814

'Redstick' Muskogee warriors defeated by combined US and Cherokee force at Horshoe bend

1816–18

First Seminole War

1819

Florida acquired from Spain.

1821

Sequoyah invents Cherokee syballary

1822

Red Cloud born

1830

Indian Removal Act requires displacement of Eastern Indians to Indian Territory (present-day Oklahoma)

1831
Sitting Bull born

1832
Black Hawk's War between US and Fox and Sauk

1835
Minority of Cherokee leaders sign Treaty of Echota

1837
Smallpox epidemic devastates tribes of the West, including the Mandan, of whom only 39 survive

1838–9
30,000 Cherokee driven from Georgia to Indian Territory along 'Trail of Tears'; the Chickasaw, Creek, Choctaw and other tribes are also relocated

1842
Seminole, last of the free tribes of the Southeast, end their guerrilla war and agree to removal from Florida, although some scattered bands remain to fight a Third Seminole War; Oregon Trail established from Independence, Missouri, to Pacific Northwest with branch to California

1848
James W. Marshall discovers gold at Sutter's Mill, California

1849
Gold Rush to California begins

1851
Indian Appropriation Act leads to reservation system becoming widespread

1860
Paiute War in Nevada

1861
Civil War (until 1865)

1862
Battle of Apache Pass between California Volunteers and Apache under Cochise and Mangas Coloradas; Homestead Act gives US citizens over 21 the right to 160 acres of public domain; Little Crow leads uprising of Santee Sioux in Minnesota, which is eventually defeated at Wood Lake

1863–4
Manuelito leads Navajo War

1864
Following their surrender, the Navajos make the 'Long Walk' to Bosque Redondo; Comanche fight Kit Carson in battle of Adobe Walls in Texas Panhandle; Colorado Volunteers massacre peaceful camp of Cheyennes and Arapahos at Sand Creek

1866
The Five Civilized Tribes forced to cede western section of Indian Territory in reprisal for some members' support of the Confederacy during Civil War; Fort Laramie Council between US government and Northern Plains tribes; Red Cloud's Sioux ambush US army near Fort Phil Kearny on Bozeman Trail in 'Fetterman Massacre'

1867
Medicine Lodge Treaty assigns reservations to Cheyennes, Arapahos, Kiowas, Kiowa-Apaches and Commanches

1868
US abandons forts on Bozeman Trail in tacit admittance of defeat in 'Red Cloud's War'; Roman Nose of Cheyenne dies in skirmish with volunteer scouts at Beecher Island ('The

Fight in Which Roman Nose Died'); George A. Custer and 7th Cavalry massacre Black Kettle's Cheyenne near Washita River, Indian Territory, in Southern Plains War

1869
Trans-continental railroad completed; Ely Parker of the Seneca appointed Indian Commissioner; first Ghost Dance movement involves tribes of Great Basin and West Coast

1870s
First recorded use of peyote amongst Indians of the US (the Lipan Apache)

1871
Congress passes law-depriving tribes of their status as separate nations

1872–4
Modoc War in lava beds of Northern California sees 165 Indians led by Captain Jack stand off vastly superior US force until artillery usage forces Modoc capitulation

1874
Cochise of the Apache dies; Comanche and allies under leadership of Quanah Parker attack buffalo hunters at Adobe Walls but are repelled by superior Sharps rifle in Red River War

1875
Quanah Parker of the Quahadi Comanche agrees to enter reservation

1876
Black Hills War begins after gold miners invade Sioux lands; Custer and 7th Cavalry defeated at Little Big Horn

1877

After a relentless campaign by US army Crazy Horse of the Sioux ceases hostilities but is killed in custody two months later; Chief Joseph's band of Nez Percé surrender after fighting for nearly 1000 miles in bid to flee to Canada

1878-9

Flight of the Northern Cheyennes from Indian Territory

1879

Carlise School founded in Penyslvania to assimilate Indians into white society

1881

Sitting Bull, Sioux victor of Little Big Horn, surrenders to US forces after leaving exile in Canada

1882

Indian Rights Association formed

1885

Sitting Bull joins Buffalo Bill's Wild West Show

1886

General Nelson A. Miles accepts the surrender of Apache warriors led by Geronimo

1887

Dawes Act divides reservations into individual holdings and opens millions of acres to white settlement

1889

First land rush into Oklahoma, formerly Indian Territory

1890

Sioux Ghost Dancers massacred by units of the 7th Cavalry at Wounded Knee, South Dakota; Indians at nearby Pine Ridge reservation flee in panic, December; Census records the Indian population as 248,253 and announces end of the frontier

January 1891
Sioux refugees surrender to Nelson Miles and return to Pine Ridge

1893
Buffalo almost extinct, only 1000 remain on Plains

1900
Indian population down to 237,000

1909
Geronimo dies

1910
Indian population of US creeps up to 277,000

1913
'The Navajo War'

1915
'The Ute War'

1916
Ishi, the last surviving member of the Yahi band of California, dies

1918
Native American Church founded

1922
John Collier founds the American Indian Defence Association

1924
Indian Citizenship Act passed

1934
Indian Reorganization Act passed, part of Roosevelt's 'New Deal' for Native Americans

1935
Last of the 'Bronco Apaches' gives up the old free life in the Sierra Madre

1941–5
25,000 Native Americans see active service with US forces during World War II

1944
National Congress of American Indians founded in Denver

1946
US Congress begins to implement 'termination' and 'relocation' policies

1968
American Indian Movement founded; Kiowa N. Scott Momaday publishes *House Made of Dawn*, which wins Pulitzer Prize for Literature in following year

1969–71
Indian militants occupy Alcatraz Island

1970
US president Richard Nixon formally repudiates termination

1972
'Trail of Broken Treaties' protest ends in occupation of the Bureau of Indian Affairs, Washington DC

1973
Activists from American Indian Movement and local Oglala Sioux stage armed protest at Wounded Knee ('Wounded Knee II')

1974

Indian Financing Act passed by US Congress

1975

Indian Self-Determination and Education Assistance Act passed; the sacred Blue Lake returned to Taos Pueblo

1978

American Indian Religious Freedom Act passed

1979

Seminole open 1700-seat bingo parlour

1981

President Reagan cuts funds for Indian social programmes by 40 per cent

1990

Native American Graves Protection and Repatriation Act passed

2000

Census records four million Americans who classify themselves as 'Native Americans'

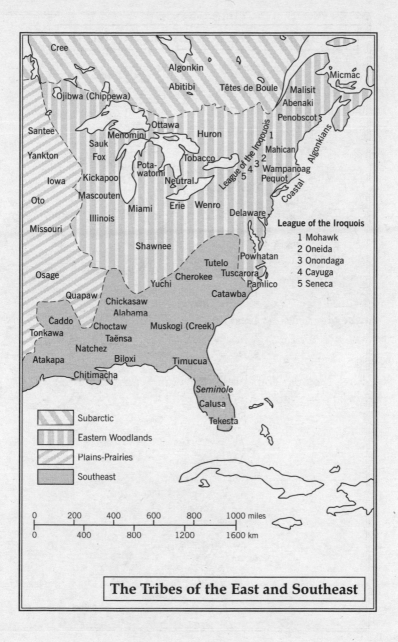

The Tribes of the East and Southeast

League of the Iroquois
1 Mohawk
2 Oneida
3 Onondaga
4 Cayuga
5 Seneca

Subarctic
Eastern Woodlands
Plains-Prairies
Southeast

0   200   400   600   800   1000 miles
0   400   800   1200   1600 km

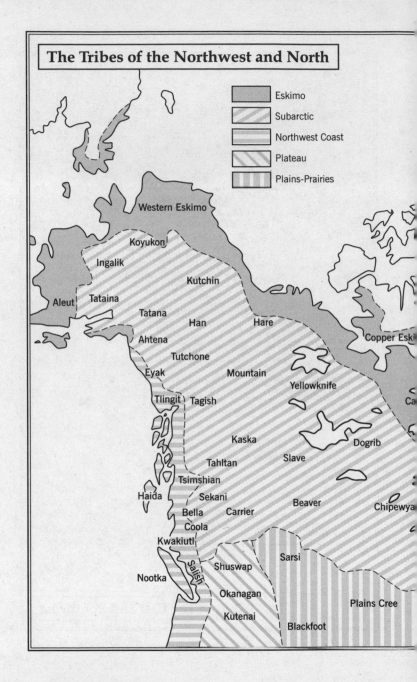

The Tribes of the Northwest and North

Legend:
- Eskimo
- Subarctic
- Northwest Coast
- Plateau
- Plains-Prairies

Western Eskimo

Koyukon

Ingalik

Kutchin

Aleut   Tataina

Tatana

Han   Hare

Copper Eski

Ahtena

Tutchone

Eyak

Mountain

Tlingit   Tagish

Yellowknife

Ca

Kaska

Dogrib

Tahltan   Slave

Tsimshian

Haida   Sekani

Bella   Carrier   Beaver   Chipewya

Coola

Kwakiutl

Salish

Sarsi

Nootka

Shuswap

Okanagan

Plains Cree

Kutenai

Blackfoot

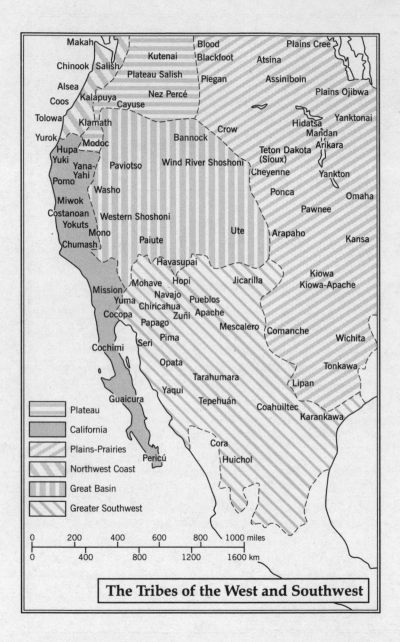

Makah
Chinook / Salish
Alsea
Coos
Tolowa
Yurok
Hupa
Yuki
Yana-
Yahi
Pomo
Miwok
Costanoan
Yokuts
Mono
Chumash
Kalapuya
Cayuse
Klamath
Modoc
Washo
Western Shoshoni
Mission
Yuma
Cocopa
Cochimi
Guaicura
Pericú

Blood
Kutenai
Blackfoot
Plateau Salish
Piegan
Nez Percé
Bannock
Crow
Wind River Shoshoni
Paviotso
Paiute
Ute
Havasupai
Mohave
Hopi
Navajo
Chiricahua
Pueblos
Zuñi
Apache
Papago
Mescalero
Pima
Seri
Opata
Tarahumara
Yaqui
Tepehuán
Cora
Huichol

Plains Cree
Atsina
Assiniboin
Plains Ojibwa
Yanktonai
Hidatsa
Mandan
Arikara
Teton Dakota
(Sioux)
Cheyenne
Yankton
Ponca
Omaha
Pawnee
Arapaho
Kansa
Kiowa
Kiowa-Apache
Jicarilla
Comanche
Wichita
Tonkawa
Lipan
Coahuiltec
Karankawa

Plateau
California
Plains-Prairies
Northwest Coast
Great Basin
Greater Southwest

0   200   400   600   800   1000 miles
0   400   800   1200   1600 km

The Tribes of the West and Southwest

Introduction

The bright winter's day of 29 December 1890. A detachment of the 7th Cavalry – Custer's regiment – stand guard over huddled, refugee Sioux. Yellow Bird, a Sioux shaman, throws a handful of dirt in the air.

The itchy-fingered cavalry open fire, killing perhaps three hundred Sioux.

Such, in synopsis, was the "battle" of Wounded Knee. As everyone knows, not least because of Dee Brown's epic *Bury My Heart at Wounded Knee*, at that remote creek in Montana occurred the last engagement in the "Indian Wars". Alongside the Sioux in the mud was killed a dream: the dream of Indian freedom.

That much is true, but Wounded Knee has come to overshadow as much as it lights, and all its symbolisms have become lop-sided. Against prevailing assumption, the story of Native Americans did not end at Wounded Knee, just as it did not begin in 1854 when the Sioux became embroiled in an argument over a white emigrant's cow on the Oregon Trail.

For too long, the history of the aboriginals of the US has become synonymous with the extended death of the Plains Indians. What of the stone cities of the ancient Anasazi? The political democracy of the 15th century Iroquois? And the struggle of the eastern tribes against the Anglo-Americans? The bloodiest conflict between Indians and Whites was not out on the Great Plains, but in the woods of New England when King Philip (Metacom) warred against the Puritans in 1675.

Moreover, America's natives have endured some of their hardest struggles *after* 1890 – against their population freefall to 250,000 in 1900, against government-sponsored "termination" in the 1950s, against subsistence existence on the reservations in the 1980s (when unemployment regularly topped 80% at Pine Ridge). In 1890, the Indians of the United States might have dropped their Remingtons and their warclubs, but they still sought control of their destiny. When, in the 1970s, Indian activists took up the "peacepath" to legally challenge treaty iniquities, their goal was the same as, say, Red Cloud's a hundred years before. Only the means differed.

There's something else about Wounded Knee. Just as it was one episode among a million in the thirty thousand-year-history of the Indians of the US, it was also an absolutely typical encounter between Whites and Natives. When Yellow Bird threw his dust in the air, he was making a Ghost Dance motion. The 7th Cavalry believed it to be a signal for the Sioux to attack them. Ever since the Europeans landed in the "New World" in 1492, their relations with the Indians have been based on misunderstanding, fear and prejudice.

Despite the best effort of some Whites, the prevailing Euro-American opinion concerning America's aboriginals over the last half-millennium is that they were ne'er-do-well "savages" who inconveniently squatted on desirous land, from which they should be removed. Sometimes this was done by force;

usually the White's microbes did the job anyway. Something like a viral holocaust descended on post-Columbian America. As much as 90% of the old population was wiped from the face of the "New World" by disease and its faithful attendant, famine.

To the more romantically minded – or just plain further removed – America's first inhabitants were sometimes conjured as "noble savages", free spirits in human form. Whether "savage savage" or "noble savage" the Indian was reduced to stereotype. Unfortunately, time has done little to diminish such impluses by Whites. You only have to consider the New Age veneration of Native culture as being the epitome of "greenness" to see that. Although well-intentioned, the New Agers have simply made another stereotype. Native cultures varied considerably, and many were distinctly politically incorrect (cannibalism and a profligate overstocking of horses which literally ate and drank *bos bison americanus* out of existence in some places, for example).

And so to this history of the Indians of the United States. In its writing, I have tried to avoid the pitfalls adumbrated above. I have tried to remember that the first Americans had a way of life as well as a way of death, that their story is long and continuing, and that it is only the White convenience that catergorises them as "Indians". To themselves, they were and are 500 different nations, composed of millions of individuals. Where possible I have let these individuals speak for themselves.

When the old and defeated Fox and Sauk chief Black Hawk met President Andrew Jackson, he declared "I am a man, and you are another". This has been my guiding sentiment on the long trail of pages which follow.

Jon E. Lewis

PART I

A World Made of Dawn

Native America, from Creation until AD 1492

Pleasant it looked
this newly created world.
Along the entire length and breadth
of the earth, our grandmother,
extended the green reflection
of her covering
and the escaping odors were pleasant to inhale

Winnebago song

From *In the Trail of the Wind*, John Bierhorst.
Copyright © 1971 John Bierhorst